ISRAEL
Land of Promise

ISRAEL
Land of Promise

ARTHUR TCHOLAKIAN

STEIN AND DAY/Publishers/New York

First published in 1973
Copyright © 1973 by Arthur Tcholakian
Library of Congress Catalog Card No. 73-79133
All rights reserved
Published simultaneously in Canada by Saunders of Toronto, Ltd.
Designed by David Miller
Printed in the United States of America
Stein and Day/*Publishers*/7 East 48 Street, New York, N.Y. 10017
ISBN 0-8128-1601-3

To my beloved daughter,
Arpiné Tcholakian, age nine;
and to my parents,
Akpar and Antaram,
who gave me birth
in Jerusalem.

I feel the Mediterranean breeze, cool and exhilarating.

The sky is full with sun.

I am in Israel, the land of my birth. A new nation is emerging—boldly, stepping out of infancy—a land of hope and prosperity for a people fighting for their heritage and space to live.

The book that I have produced hopefully reflects the realities of a country experiencing manifold transitions. It is with an intense emotional attachment that I have attempted to capture the images of these proud people of fierce hope and determination; a people steadfast in their commitment to control their own sovereign destiny.

Arthur Tcholakian

David Ben-Gurion,

Israel's first premier, looking out on the city of Jerusalem

Premier Golda Meir

Defense Minister Moshe Dayan

The tomb of Theodor Herzl, founder of modern Zionism, in Jerusalem

Memorial to the heroes
of the 1948 War of
Liberation on the
road to Jerusalem

Members of Israeli defense forces

Women's army recruits

First days in the army

Women serve twenty months in the army

Defense Minister Moshe Dayan at his office

Lt. Col. Dov Raviv, training base commander

Lt. Gen. David (Dado) Elazar, Chief of Staff

Orientation

From many nations...

...soldiers of Israel

Israel's defense forces play a vital role in the life of the young nation

*An extensive reserve system enables Israel to mobilize
rapidly when attacked*

The army is also a social experience

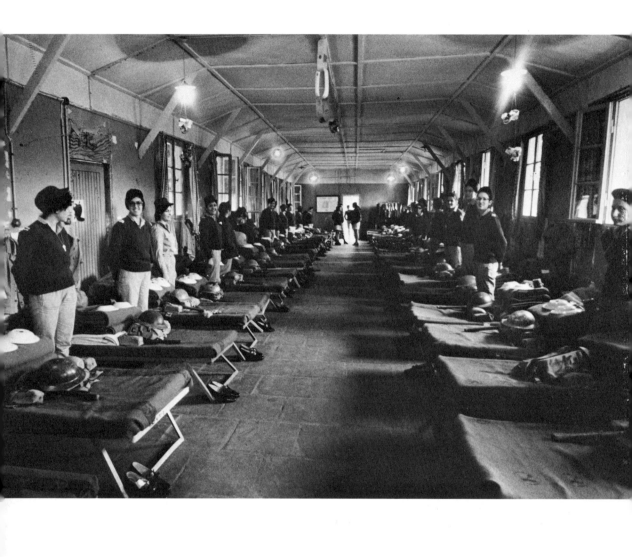

Women's army training discipline includes use of light arms

Irrigation and fertilization make arid lands arable

President Zalman Shazar

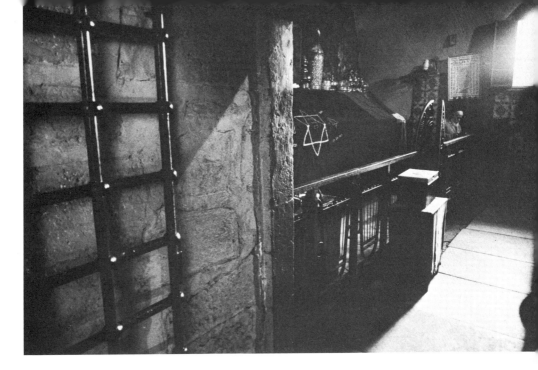

The tomb of King David on Mt. Zion

Portion of the Dead Sea Scrolls

Foreign Minister Abba Eban

Shlomo Yosef Burg, Minister of the Interior

The kibbutz, or collective farming settlement, was a

key factor in the establishment of modern Israel

Members, volunteers, and

children live and work on a cooperative basis

Pinhas Sapier, Minister of Finance

Shimon Peres, Minister of Transport and Communications

Hitch-hiking is a way of life

M. Zanbar, Governor of the Bank of Israel

Israel exports a wide range of agricultural, industrial,
and consumer goods

Metals and raw materials are mined and processed for
domestic and foreign consumption

Four thousand years of history

Raphael Levy, District Commissioner of Jerusalem

City of Jerusalem

Teddy Kollek, Mayor of Jerusalem

Ritual objects for sale in a souvenir shop indicate Israel's ancient religious tradition

Menorah sculpture in the Israel Museum complex in Jerusalem, with the Knesset, Israel's Parliament, in background

Magen Broshi, curator of the Shrine of the Book

The Shrine of the Book where the Dead Sea Scrolls are housed

The Western Wall in Jerusalem, the most holy site in Judaism

Children in Mea Shearim, the Orthodox quarter of Jerusalem

In Mea Shearim

Jews and Arabs mingle in Jerusalem

Shlomo Goren,
Chief Ashkenazi Rabbi of Israel

Moslems and Christians, as well as Jews, live in modern Israel

An ancient art and an ancient trade

Urban congestion has come to Jerusalem and other Israeli cities

Education until the age of fourteen is compulsory

More than fifty thousand
students are enrolled at
Israel's six universities

Tel Aviv University

Haifa University

Magen David Adom, Israel's Red Cross, maintains clinics

throughout the country

Arab school children in Gaza

Jerusalem, holy to many faiths

"You are my wife according to the Law of Moses"

Lod International Airport

The new

Israelis

*One third of
Israel's three million
people are under
the age of fifteen*

The Sea of Galilee

Raanan Levi, a young artist

Painter Reuven Rubin and his wife

A fisherman

The Mediterranean Sea

Tel Aviv

Haifa

A general view of Tel Aviv from Shalom Tower

Western influences persist

Yehoshua Rabinovitz, Mayor of Tel Aviv

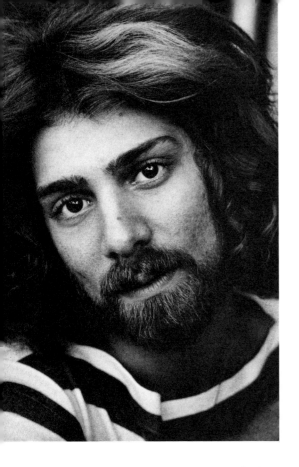

Cafe society

Mrs. Sara Tadmor

Mrs. Esther Rubin

Nation's leaders attend the funeral of Kadish Luz, former

Speaker of the Knesset . . .

THE TEL AVIV MUSEUM מוזיאון תל אביב

Mrs. Haim Gamzu briefs visitors to the Tel Aviv Museum

David Ben-Gurion

"An independent nation in its own land..."

ABOUT THE AUTHOR

Arthur Tcholakian is an Armenian immigrant to America who became a naturalized citizen in 1964. For more than a decade, he worked in New York as an advertising and fashion photographer. In 1969, at the height of his career, Tcholakian dropped his commercial undertakings to devote his time to more expressive themes.

The first of these, *The Majesty of the Black Woman*, was completed in 1970 and represents fifteen months of concentrated effort. One critic hailed Tcholakian's statement as "the first positive and optimistic work about black Americans ever produced in this country."

Tcholakian next hurled himself into a second extended project, this time a two-year photographic study of the life and folkways of the Republic of Armenia. One of the first American photographers to become intimately acquainted with the leaders of the Soviet politbureau, he accompanied and photographed Party Chief and First Secretary Leonid Brezhnev on the occasion of the fiftieth anniversary of the Armenian state. *The Armenian SSR: State, People, Life* is to be published in the near future.

For his current work, *Israel: Land of Promise*, Tcholakian returned to the land where in 1928 he was born of Armenian parents. Intensely involved in this major project, he journeyed to all part of Israel —from Jerusalem to Tel-Aviv, Haifa, Acre, Sinai, and Golan Heights.

At the conclusion of Tcholakian's photographic session at the Ministry of Defense in Tel-Aviv, Moshe Dayan commented to him, "Your spirit of working is like ours—undefeatable."